Original title:
Verses in Stone

Copyright © 2024 Creative Arts Management OÜ
All rights reserved.

Author: Tim Wood
ISBN HARDBACK: 978-9916-88-110-1
ISBN PAPERBACK: 978-9916-88-111-8

The Weight of Words in Granite

Words carved deep, in silence stay,
Chiseled thoughts of time's decay.
Whispers linger in the stone,
Heavy truths, forever known.

Echoes of a past debate,
Each letter holds a twist of fate.
Voices trapped in fleeting trace,
Silent witnesses, we embrace.

Chronicles of the Earth's Silence

Mountains rise with quiet grace,
Guardians of this timeless place.
Caverns deep, where shadows speak,
Nature's secrets softly seek.

In stillness lies a hidden tale,
Of whispered winds that seldom wail.
The earth breathes slow, its stories old,
In quietude, the past unfolds.

Stories Borne from Rugged Formations

Rocky cliffs and valleys wide,
Hold the tales that time can't hide.
Each fracture tells of storms once faced,
In their scars, life is traced.

Waves and winds shape every line,
Nature's hand, a grand design.
From rugged faces, legends grow,
In silent valleys, echoes flow.

Ancient Echoes within the Stone

Beneath the earth, whispers sound,
Echoes of ages lost, profound.
Fossils rest, time's silent themes,
Woven deep in ancient dreams.

With every grain, the past survives,
Stories linger, as time thrives.
In the stillness, we find a home,
In ancient echoes, we softly roam.

Ancient Scripts of the Land

In the soil whispers old tales,
Winds carry secrets on their gales.
Roots entwine with forgotten lore,
Each grain a memory, rich and store.

By rivers deep, stones hold their peace,
Echoes of laughter that never cease.
Time's gentle hand in every crease,
Nature writes history with skillful ease.

Silent Odes of the Mountain Pass

Silent peaks rise under the sun,
Chanting softly when day is done.
Echoes linger in the crisp air,
Breathing life into dreams we dare.

The snow-capped crowns, regal and bright,
Guarding the paths, both day and night.
Every trail holds a whispered sound,
Of journeys made and lost then found.

Stone Auras of Forgotten Words

In the cool shadow of ancient trees,
Crumbled stones tell tales with ease.
Characters etched, worn yet bold,
Guardians of tales that must be told.

Beneath the moss, history sleeps,
In whispers soft, the past still keeps.
Lingering gently in the twilight haze,
Stone auras gleam in the evening's gaze.

Murmurs of the Rocky Outcrop

On the outcrop where shadows play,
Murmurs of time linger and sway.
Every crack and crevice sounds,
With stories of life that nature crowns.

The wind carries echoes of old,
In the heart of the rock, memories held.
Listen closely, for you'll discern,
The whispers of ages in each turn.

The Foundation of Lost Songs

In echoes where the shadows play,
Whispers of the past drift away.
Notes forgotten, in silence thrive,
Through stillness, their memories strive.

Harmonies buried beneath the ground,
In every pulse, a heartbeat found.
Melodies lost in the winds of time,
Lost songs yearning for a rhyme.

Unearthing Silent Histories

Buried deep, the stories wait,
In layers thick, fate left to fate.
Silent tales of ancient skies,
In every grain, a truth that lies.

Hands that dig through earth's embrace,
Revealing paths, a vivid trace.
Forgotten lives in shadows bloom,
Unraveling threads in the hidden room.

Layers of Life in the Limestone

From ancient seas, the stones arise,
Captured echoes of nature's cries.
Layer by layer, the past reveals,
The pulse of life that earth conceals.

Calcium tales in every stratum,
A testament to what came at 'em.
Veins of time in a solid wall,
Whispering secrets to those who'll call.

Nature's Manuscript in Solid Form

In stone engravings, stories penned,
Nature's lore, without an end.
Every crack, a narrative known,
In every ridge, a journey shown.

Chronicles etched in solid ground,
Where wisdom in silence is found.
Molecules merging through endless reign,
Nature's script in a timeless chain.

From Grain to Granite

From grain that shifts in gentle breeze,
Roots reach deep, anchored with ease.
Time sculpts a form, rugged and true,
Nature's hand carves, creates anew.

Through storms that rage and sun that burns,
The mountain stands, as the world turns.
Layers of history etched in stone,
Silent witnesses, never alone.

In valleys deep where shadows creep,
The whispers of ages, secrets to keep.
From grains of sand to peaks so grand,
The journey spans a timeless land.

Each boulder holds a tale of old,
In every crack, a story told.
From grain to granite, we rise and fall,
In nature's realm, we answer the call.

The Stony Songs of Ages

In ancient quarries, echoes play,
Stony songs where shadows sway.
Through ages passed, their voices ring,
A symphony of earth, forever sing.

With every chip and every crack,
The stones remember, never lack.
Whispers lost, but found again,
In every rock, a tale of men.

The winds entwine through canyon walls,
In every crevice, history calls.
Time's gentle hand leaves marks unseen,
In stony songs, our hearts convene.

Each river's course, each mountain's peak,
In silent tones, the ancients speak.
The stony songs of ages vast,
In every moment, the world amassed.

Echoing Whispers of Stone

In caverns deep where echoes dwell,
The whispers of stone cast a spell.
Nature's breath in muted tones,
The heart of the mountain, carved in bones.

From crystal caves to weathered cliffs,
Each whisper holds a tale that drifts.
Through fissures wide, the secrets flow,
A dance of silence, softly aglow.

With each rumble, a story shared,
In the heart of stone, moments dared.
The echoes carry both joy and pain,
A melody sweet, a haunting refrain.

Under starlit skies, shadows blend,
Whispers of stone that never end.
In silent watch, they guard the night,
Echoing softly, holding light.

Carvings of the Forgotten

In shadows deep, where whispers dwell,
Old stone tells tales of time's soft spell.
Figures carved with hands of grace,
Lost voices echo in this place.

Forgotten dreams beneath the moss,
The artist's touch, a heavy cost.
Each groove holds stories, long since shared,
Among the stones, they persevere.

Etched in the Heart of the Mountain

High among the peaks, so bold,
Nature's script in rocks of old.
Lines of wisdom carved with care,
Secrets breathed in the mountain air.

Each fissure tells of storms and grace,
A timeless dance, a slow embrace.
Here the earth keeps its own score,
Echoes of ages rest at its core.

Miracles in the Quarry Dust

In swirling dust, such wonders play,
Chisels strike as night turns gray.
Lifetimes born from grit and strife,
Beauty emerges, shaping life.

Every chip a whispered sigh,
Formed from dreams that never die.
In dusty air, hope's seeds are sown,
Crafted by hands, so wild, alone.

Secrets of the Moonlit Rock

Underneath the silver hue,
Silent stones hold secrets true.
In the night they start to glow,
Stories hidden deep below.

Whispering winds through ancient trees,
Unravel tales upon the breeze.
The moonlight casts its gentle spell,
Where the rock and shadows dwell.

The Hand of Time in Solid Form

In shadows cast by ancient stone,
The timeworn whispers softly moan.
Each grain a tale, a life once lived,
In chiseled silence, secrets hid.

As ages pass, the echoes fade,
Yet in each crack, a memory laid.
With every touch, we feel its grip,
The hand of time, an endless trip.

In the Heart of the Quarry's Voice

Deep within the rocky maze,
A voice resounds through endless days.
It sings of labor, toil, and grace,
Each echo finds a hollow space.

The hammer strikes, the dust will rise,
From earth to rock, beneath the skies.
In every shift, a story flows,
In quarry's heart, the spirit grows.

Stones that Whisper Stories

Beneath the weight of ages past,
The stones stand firm, their shadows cast.
Each fissure tells of storms endured,
In whispered tones, their tales secured.

Listen close, let silence speak,
In every crack, their voices leak.
From mountain high to valley floor,
The stones will share what's left in store.

A Tapestry of Earth's Memories

Woven threads of earth's embrace,
In every fold, a sacred space.
From roots that anchor to the sky,
A tapestry where moments lie.

The rivers carve, the winds adorn,
Each element, a story born.
In hues of green, in shades of gray,
A masterpiece both night and day.

Echoing Silence

In the depths where shadows dwell,
Quiet whispers weave a spell.
Lost in thoughts, the heart takes flight,
In echoing silence, we find light.

Dreams entwined in midnight air,
Fragile hopes, a whispered prayer.
Each moment deep with untold grace,
Absorbing stillness, soft embrace.

The world outside begins to fade,
In this realm, no masquerade.
Time stands still, the stars align,
Within the silence, truth we find.

Beneath the stars, we sit in peace,
In solitude, our burdens cease.
Echoes linger, softly call,
In echoing silence, we stand tall.

The Dance of the Stone

Ancient boulders, weathered grace,
In nature's arms, they find their place.
Through ages passed, they learn to sway,
In the dance of the stone, they play.

Mountains rise with steady pride,
Silent witnesses, they bide.
Roots and veins, their stories told,
In every crack, a memory bold.

Seasons change, yet they remain,
Their steadfast hearts, a quiet reign.
Cascading waters, soft and free,
Join the stones in their reverie.

In twilight's glow, they come alive,
In harmony, the spirits thrive.
Together swaying, they enthrone,
The timeless beauty of the stone.

Artifacts of the Soul

Hidden treasures, thoughts out loud,
Whispers lost within the crowd.
Each experience, a precious gem,
Artifacts of the soul, we stem.

Memories etched in cloth and clay,
Stories woven in night and day.
Hearts entangled, forever bound,
In the silence, our truths are found.

Time's gentle hand, it leaves its mark,
In shadows deep, it sparks a spark.
Every laugh, each tear we've known,
The artifacts we call our own.

From shadows cast, our stories glow,
Past and present, a seamless flow.
In the gallery, we stand whole,
Celebrating artifacts of the soul.

Remnants of the Past

Whispers linger in the air,
Faded echoes whisper care.
Memories dance in twilight's glow,
Remnants of the past we know.

Time has painted shadows long,
In every heart, a secret song.
Fragile moments caught in time,
Remnants of the past, we climb.

Each footstep laid upon the soil,
A journey rich, an endless toil.
Through hidden paths, we trace the line,
To find the roots where we can shine.

In the quiet, lessons rest,
In the echoes, we get blessed.
For every tale that we outlast,
We cherish still, the past amassed.

Echoes Beneath the Surface

Whispers dance in quiet depths,
Ripples mirror faded dreams.
Lost voices linger, soft and low,
Carried on the silent streams.

In shadows where the secrets hide,
Time weaves tales in watery threads.
Beneath the stillness, stories thrive,
Echoes of all that once was said.

Fingers trace the cool, wet stone,
Tracing paths of ancient lore.
Every drop a memory,
In the depths, we seek for more.

Beneath the surface, life resides,
Awakened by the light above.
In echoes, we find our truth,
In silence, we discover love.

Treasures of the Quarry

Deep within the rocky heart,
Glimmers hide in dark embrace.
Each fragment holds a story told,
Of toil, of time, of grace.

Chisels sing their rhythmic song,
As miners craft from stone to dream.
Every layer, every crack,
Holds secrets whispered in the beam.

Rough edges shape the tender soul,
Beauty born from ancient ground.
In every treasure, a journey,
In silence, a voice is found.

In the quarry, nature's will,
Carved by hands with purpose true.
From earth to light, creation's breath,
In every shard, a world anew.

Portraits in Pebble

Tiny stones with stories vast,
Whittled down by wind and wave.
Each one holds a piece of time,
A memory of land and brave.

Glistening under sunbeam's kiss,
Colors swirl in nature's art.
In the smallest pebble's form,
Lies a universe to impart.

Children gather them in hands,
Creating worlds from what they find.
In their laughter, echoes blend,
With the rhythm of the kind.

Portraits crafted, simple, true,
Nature's beauty, small yet grand.
In each pebble, life's embrace,
Stories forged from sea and sand.

The Resonance of Ruins

Stones that breathe of days long past,
Whisper tales in the twilight glow.
Architecture bent by time,
Halls where shadows softly flow.

Columned faces watch the sky,
Old arches cradle silent dreams.
Each crack and crevice speaks of loss,
In the stillness, history gleams.

Moss blankets where once stood proud,
Nature's brush reclaiming ground.
In the ruins, life persists,
In decay, beauty is found.

The resonance of ancient stone,
Echoes haunt both night and day.
In the whispers of the past,
The present learns to find its way.

Echoed Emotions in Quarried Rock

In silence deep, the shadows dance,
Whispers of time in a fleeting glance.
Carved by hands that sought to seek,
Echoed truths in the stone we speak.

Grains of dust tell tales of old,
Secrets buried, legends bold.
Chisel strikes with rhythmic beat,
Fossils of feelings beneath our feet.

Worn and weathered, yet they stand,
Monuments to the artist's hand.
Each chip released, a story told,
In quarried rock, our hearts unfold.

Nature's grip in crags we find,
A reflection of the human mind.
In every slab, emotions flow,
Art and earth and time bestow.

From the Depths of the Earth

Beneath the soil, the silence fears,
A world of whispers, cries and tears.
Roots entwined with ancient stone,
The pulse of earth, a heart unknown.

In caverns dark, where echoes fade,
Visions linger, memories made.
Crystals glisten, secrets kept,
In depths uncharted, dreams are wept.

The weight of time, a heavy shroud,
Voices linger, soft yet loud.
From fiery core to surface air,
Resilience blooms, a tale to share.

Through tunnels carved, life's journey flows,
A tapestry of highs and lows.
From the depths, we rise anew,
In earthy veins, our spirits brew.

Stone Palaces of the Mind

Within our thoughts, grand castles rise,
Wrought from dreams and hidden sighs.
Each chamber holds a different door,
Unlocking wonders, forevermore.

Stone towers reach for starlit skies,
A fortress built where silence lies.
In halls of light, our hopes entwine,
Immortal echoes weave the line.

With every step, the echoes sigh,
Whispers tethered to the sky.
Each pathway paved with memories,
A labyrinth of heartfelt pleas.

The throne of thought, a sacred place,
Carved from time and gentle grace.
Stone palaces where visions gleam,
In the mind's heart, we dream our dream.

Unraveled Threads of Nature's Tapestry

In nature's loom, the colors blend,
Threads of life that twist and bend.
Each fiber tells a story rich,
In woven strands, a sacred hitch.

Gentle breezes shift the yarn,
Sunshine ribbons, bright and warm.
Mountains cradle, streams embrace,
A tapestry of time and space.

From dawn to dusk, the patterns shift,
With every season, nature's gift.
Patterns drawn with delicate grace,
Unraveled threads in sacred place.

In every stitch, a tale resides,
Woven deeply where truth abides.
Nature's art, both bold and shy,
Unraveled threads, forever lie.

Solidify My Dreams

In the hush of night, I sow,
Fleeting thoughts begin to grow.
Stars above shall guide my way,
As I chase the break of day.

Each whisper holds a promise true,
In the moonlight, dreams renew.
With every heartbeat, I will soar,
To touch the skies and seek for more.

A canvas bright, my visions gleam,
Painting life, the perfect theme.
With courage vast, I set my sail,
To solidify my dreams, prevail.

These hopes, like fire, fiercely burn,
In the dance of fate, I yearn.
With vision clear, I press ahead,
In the tale of life, I'll be led.

Memories Grasped in Stone

In gentle hands, the past resides,
Whispers echo, love abides.
In every chisel, every mark,
A story waits in shadows dark.

Carved in stone, a timeless scheme,
Fragments of a distant dream.
Moments held in granite's grace,
In stillness, time finds its place.

Each sculpted line, a heartbeat stored,
In silence, memories restored.
Through ages vast, they speak so bold,
Stories etched, and truths unfold.

With every crack, a tale of old,
In the light, their warmth behold.
Memories grasped, forever shine,
In the realm where hearts entwine.

Footprints Eternally Carved

Through shifting sands, we leave our mark,
Footprints fade, yet echo spark.
Each step we take, a journey spun,
In the dance of life, we're one.

With every stride, the earth it sings,
Tales of joy and woes it brings.
Eternal paths that intertwine,
In the fabric of space and time.

These prints will stand through storm and sun,
In the hearts of those, we're never done.
Stories woven through sand and stone,
Footprints left, we are not alone.

In shadows cast, our lives unfold,
Paths of warmth, and memories bold.
In this world, we'll ever chart,
Eternally carved, the soul's true heart.

Carving Time's Narrative

In the tender hands of fate,
Time unfolds and we create.
Chiseling dreams with every breath,
Crafting life, defying death.

With every moment, stories flow,
In the light, our hopes will grow.
Chronicles of laughter, tears,
Carving out the span of years.

Time's swift passage, a sculptor wise,
Shapes our lives beneath the skies.
In strokes of fate, we find our way,
A narrative spun, come what may.

In whispers soft, time's magic speaks,
In every heart, a story seeks.
With every dawn, a new chance to rise,
Carving time's narrative under wise skies.

Fossils of Emotion

In the silence of the past,
Whispers of hearts long gone,
Trapped in layers of time,
Echoes of love still drawn.

Beneath the weight of sorrow,
Memories etched in stone,
Every crack tells a story,
Of paths we walked alone.

Dusty dreams lie buried,
In a field of fading light,
Unearthed by gentle fingers,
Revealed in the soft night.

Fossils of our laughter,
Hardened under the sun,
Reminders of our essence,
In time, we're never done.

Granite Harmonies

Rocks in silence pondering,
Ancient tales carved in stone,
Each grain a distant echo,
Where dreams were sown and grown.

Mountains hum a soft tune,
Winds carry the melody,
Nature's voice a symphony,
Stirring hearts wild and free.

In shadows, shadows tremble,
Notes held in the cool breeze,
Granite harmonies linger,
Whispering through the trees.

Time may chip every surface,
Yet souls remain entwined,
In the heart of the mountain,
Where our spirits aligned.

The Rhyme of Ages

Verses lost in twilight,
Where time drifts slowly by,
Each moment finds a rhythm,
Beneath the endless sky.

Footsteps trace our stories,
In the dust of ancient days,
Every laugh and sorrow,
Composes life's long phrase.

Echoes of the yesterdays,
Sing softly in our dreams,
Each heartbeat's gentle measure,
Flows like eternal streams.

With the dawn, a new stanza,
Begins the endless dance,
Together in this rhyme,
We find our second chance.

Pillow of Earth

Nestled in the quiet soil,
Where secrets safely lie,
The roots of life entwining,
Underneath the sky.

Soft whispers fill the garden,
In every flower's bloom,
A pillow made of earth,
Cradles dreams in the loom.

Nature's gentle blanket,
Holds stories yet untold,
The warmth of life surrounding,
In colors bright and bold.

Sleep now, under starlight,
Let the earth's love embrace,
In this sacred space,
Find the peace of place.

Inscriptions of the Ancients

In deepened caves where shadows play,
Old stories breathe, not far away.
Hieroglyphs etched on weathered stone,
Whispers of lives once fully grown.

Flickering torchlight unveils the past,
Capturing moments that forever last.
Silent echoes of a time before,
Tales of glory, adventures galore.

Nature reclaims what man has wrought,
Memories linger, wisdom taught.
Beneath the dust, the truth remains,
History's burden, joys, and pains.

In every stone, a heartbeat beats,
Connecting worlds in ancient sweets.
We listen close, for we are one,
Inscriptions speak, our hearts weigh a ton.

Timeless Tales

Under the stars, stories unfold,
Whispers of magic, legends retold.
Chronicles woven in moonlit nights,
Timeless tales that take to flights.

In the forest, shadows dance,
Fables captured in wild romance.
Each leaf a chapter, every breeze,
Carrying secrets through ancient trees.

Lovers' sighs etch hearts in stone,
Failures, triumphs, we're not alone.
Each verse a window, each word a key,
Unlocking dreams of what could be.

As dawn breaks, we hold them tight,
These timeless tales, our guiding light.
For in their depths, we find our way,
Living in stories, come what may.

Chiseled Reflections

Sculpted marble, gleams and glows,
Capturing beauty that time bestows.
In every curve, a life unknown,
Chiseled reflections, dreams have grown.

A chisel strikes, intent so clear,
Revealing emotions, capturing fear.
Each crack and crevice tells a tale,
Of passions ignited, hopes that sail.

In dust and stone, we find our past,
Echoes of moments that forever last.
Carved in silence, whispers reside,
Embodying truths we cannot hide.

The sculptor's hand, a guiding force,
Molding hearts, embracing the course.
Chiseled reflections, beautiful, bright,
Remind us to cherish the fleeting light.

The Heart of Gravel

In the quiet streets, a rhythm lines,
Where gravel hugs the earth, it shines.
Every stone a story, each crack a song,
In the heart of gravel, we all belong.

Footsteps echo on paths unknown,
Journey's begun, we venture alone.
Through dust and grit, we find our way,
Learning the lessons of each new day.

Underneath the stars, dreams collide,
In the heart of gravel, we take pride.
Hope springs eternal, amidst the grey,
Shape our destinies, come what may.

Together we wander, together we grieve,
In every pebble, we learn to believe.
The heart of gravel beats strong and clear,
A testament to those we hold dear.

Corners of the Earth's Narrative

In whispers soft, the stories flow,
From mountains high to valleys low.
Ancient rocks hold secrets tight,
Each crack a tale of day and night.

Rivers weave through time's own thread,
Bridges to the past, where shadows tread.
The sky narrates in starry light,
While storms unleash their tales in flight.

Every rustle of the leaf reveals,
A history that nature feels.
Wind carries whispers from afar,
Each gust a paragraph, a memoir.

In corners quiet, the earth will speak,
Binding the lost, the soft, the meek.
Through ages vast, yet ever near,
The narrative of life appears.

Life Stilled in Earth's Embrace

In twilight's glow, the stillness reigns,
Life rests softly on the plains.
Roots cradle dreams beneath the ground,
In quietude, peace is found.

The whispers hush, the shadows blend,
Nature's lullaby, a gentle mend.
Each heartbeat echoes in the soil,
In drowsy calm, the earth will toil.

Warmth lingers in the morning dew,
As day unfolds its vibrant hue.
Time pauses in this sacred space,
Where life is held in earth's embrace.

And as the sun dips low and deep,
The world succumbs to soothing sleep.
In stillness, dreams will intertwine,
Life breathes slowly, soft and fine.

Sketches in the Sands of Time

In fleeting grains, the moments lie,
Stories written 'neath the sky.
Each footprint made, a tale untold,
Sketches shimmer in the gold.

The tides will rise, the tides will fall,
Erasing secrets, one and all.
Yet memories cling like shells to shore,
Layers of life, forevermore.

Sunset paints with hues divine,
A canvas bold, a design.
As day surrenders to starry night,
Timelines shift in the soft twilight.

In every curve of shifting sand,
Lives have danced and dreams have planned.
Fleeting moments, yet they stay,
Sketches fade but never stray.

The Heartbeat of the Core

Deep within, where shadows dwell,
A rhythm pulses, a sacred bell.
The earth's own heartbeats strong and true,
Throughout the layers, life anew.

From molten depths, volcanoes roar,
An ancient hymn, a vibrant score.
Each tremor speaks of time's embrace,
Of life emerging, taking space.

Through caverns dark and chambers bright,
The core's soft thrum ignites the night.
It whispers tales of ages past,
Of turbulent storms that fade so fast.

With every shift and every shake,
The heartbeat drives the paths we make.
In earth's deep song, we find our lore,
Connected always, forevermore.

Tales Carved in Silence

In shadows deep, where whispers lie,
The stones recall an ancient sigh.
Each crack and crevice tells a tale,
Of lost hopes and dreams that pale.

Through silent halls, the echoes roam,
In every corner, they find home.
Like breathless wind through chiseled rock,
They seek the heart, the timeless clock.

Beneath the weight of time's own hand,
The stories wait on gritty land.
Each grain a witness, strong and bold,
To secrets that the ages hold.

In twilight's glow, the stillness reigns,
While memory in silence gains.
The stones stand firm, their vigil slow,
In silence, tales of life will grow.

Memories Set in Marble

Upon the marble, smooth and bright,
Lie fragments of forgotten light.
Each polished surface, a silent plea,
Holds whispers of what used to be.

In every vein and subtle line,
A history etched, so divine.
With every touch, one feels the past,
In moments stored, our shadows cast.

The echoes of a lover's vow,
Forever frozen in the now.
Each gentle curve and fleeting trace,
Reflects the love we can't erase.

Beneath the surface, stories lie,
Like buried seeds, they yearn to fly.
In heavy stone, our hopes reside,
In memories set, there's no divide.

Legends of the Ancient Quarry

In ancient quarries, shadows play,
Where stones were born and dreams gave way.
The pick and chisel sang their song,
Of strength and struggle, never wrong.

Each boulder shaped by hands so bold,
Holds sagas of the young and old.
The echo of a miner's cheer,
Resounds within the quarry's sphere.

From darkness deep, the light does break,
As legends stir for memory's sake.
In crumbled stone, the spirits dwell,
With tales of toil, they weave their spell.

Eons pass, yet still they call,
In craggy walls, they stand for all.
The lessons learned in sweat and dust,
Are forged in time, remain in trust.

Words Wrought in Earth's Embrace

From earth's embrace, the words emerge,
In whispers low, they gently surge.
Each syllable, a grain of sand,
Crafted by nature's steady hand.

The soil holds tales of love and strife,
Of every creature's fleeting life.
In roots that weave beneath our feet,
The language of the earth is sweet.

As seasons shift, the verses grow,
In harmony with sun and snow.
The rhythm flows through every vein,
In earth's embrace, we find our gain.

With every storm that bends the trees,
New words arise upon the breeze.
In vibrant hues, the earth will sing,
Of timeless truths that nature brings.

Gazes Fixed on Enduring Walls

Stone whispers tales of old,
Secrets held in shadows bold.
Eyes that linger, hearts that feel,
Time's embrace, a steadfast seal.

Each crack a story, years unfold,
In the silence, histories told.
Bound in quiet, strength they portray,
Witnessing life, come what may.

Memories etched in every grain,
Veins of the past, a sacred chain.
Reflections dance in twilight's gleam,
Enduring walls tell our dream.

Through storms they stand, unyielding gaze,
Guardians of time, steadfast blaze.
In their presence, we find our way,
Gazes fixed on yesterday.

Layers of Time in the Gravel

Beneath our feet, stories lie,
Whispers of ages, softest sigh.
Grains of moments, lost yet found,
Layers of time on hallowed ground.

Each step a journey, echoing past,
Footprints fading, shadows cast.
Nature's canvas, rich and deep,
In the gravel, secrets keep.

Pebbles polished by the flow,
Lessons learned, a silent show.
The pressing weight of earth's sweet breath,
In layers of time, we meet our death.

So tread softly, heed the call,
For in each step, we rise and fall.
The gravel sings, a lullaby,
Layers of time beneath the sky.

Palimpsest of the Primitive Route

Footpaths worn by ancient tread,
Stories written, long since dead.
Beneath the earth, a tale unfolds,
Palimpsest of the ancient bold.

Markings faint, yet ever clear,
Echoes of those who once were here.
Nature's ink, the forest's breath,
Woven paths between life and death.

Twists and turns 'neath canopies high,
Journeys whispered where shadows lie.
Traces linger, a gentle hint,
Of lives entwined in the forest's print.

Primitive routes, a sacred thread,
In every step, the past is fed.
Every journey circles anew,
Palimpsest of the wildest view.

Timeless Etchings in Stone

Chiseled words in silent stone,
Echo through ages, never alone.
Carved by hands from long ago,
Timeless secrets, wisdom flows.

Granite heart, a steadfast soul,
Enduring stories, making us whole.
In each fissure, time's embrace,
Etchings of life in a sacred space.

Mosaic of moments, forever bound,
Under the weight of earth's profound.
Nature weaves in patterns grand,
Timeless etchings meant to stand.

So pause awhile, feel the thrill,
In stone's silence, hearts are still.
With every glance, we understand,
Timeless etchings across the land.

Stories Embedded in the Earth

Beneath the soil, secrets lie,
Whispers of ages pass by.
Roots intertwine, tales unfold,
Stone and grain, stories told.

Rivers carve through ancient lands,
Marking time with gentle hands.
Footprints fade in the dust,
History's echo, a timeless trust.

Mountains rise with silent grace,
Guardians of a sacred space.
Each layer tells of what once was,
An earthbound tale, nature's applause.

In every creak of the wood,
Lives the past, misunderstood.
Through gentle winds and soft rains,
The heart of the earth forever remains.

The Weight of Silent Echoes

In shadows cast, the voices blend,
Silent echoes, a long-lost friend.
The weight of words still lingers near,
Filling the space with what we fear.

Eyes that meet but never speak,
A longing heart, growing weak.
Moments shared, now left to roam,
Within the silence, we find our home.

The clock ticks loud, yet all is calm,
A steady pulse, a haunting psalm.
Each tick a memory, softly we bind,
In whispers of time, what's left behind.

Heavy is the heart that knows,
The song of silence, ebbing flows.
In every breath, we hold our truth,
In echoes of the unheard youth.

Chiseled Dreams Beneath the Surface

In stone and clay, our dreams reside,
Chiseled hearts, where hopes abide.
Beneath the surface, visions gleam,
In quiet moments, we dare to dream.

Crafted by hands both worn and wise,
With every carve, a new sunrise.
Layers form, histories entwined,
In every crevice, a love defined.

An artist's touch, a sculptor's grace,
Bringing life to a timeless space.
Carved in silence, pure and deep,
Dreams awaken from their sleep.

Beneath the weight of earthly shrouds,
The spirit rises, breaking clouds.
In every stone, a story beams,
Chiseled deep, alive with dreams.

Inscriptions of Time's Journey

Beneath the stars, our stories write,
Inscriptions of day, and the cloak of night.
Carved in moments, forever to last,
Tracing the footsteps of our past.

Each tick of time, a mark we leave,
Fragile threads that weaves and cleave.
In the whispers of dusk, we learn,
With every turn, our hearts still yearn.

Through valleys low and mountains high,
Time's ink flows, it will not die.
On weathered stones and fading walls,
Our legacy in silence calls.

In the eternal dance of sun and moon,
Inscriptions echo a haunting tune.
As time unfolds its woven tale,
We journey forth, where dreams prevail.

Monumental Myths

In ancient stone, the tales reside,
Of gods and heroes, side by side.
Each carving whispers, echoes past,
Their legacies in shadows cast.

Upon this rock, the battles fought,
With each chisel, history sought.
Legends rise and never fade,
In every layer, stories made.

The mountains stand, their silence deep,
Where secrets lie, the ages sleep.
From dust to dreams, the cycles flow,
Monumental myths, forever grow.

In every crease, a truth concealed,
The voice of time, a fate revealed.
Within the stone, our hearts align,
Monuments of a grand design.

Sculpted Memories

Chiseled faces in the grey,
Echoing moments, fade away.
Crafted hands, they hold the light,
In every shadow, hope shines bright.

Whispers dance on the cool, hard stone,
Fragments of lives once fully grown.
Emotions carved in fleeting time,
A silent pact, a soft chime.

Each sculpture tells a tale untold,
Of love and loss, of brave and bold.
Memories shaped through time's embrace,
In every curve, a warm trace.

As ages pass, they stand so still,
Capturing moments, hearts to fill.
Sculpted memories, a bittersweet song,
In the gallery of time, where we all belong.

Silent Sonnet

In quiet corners, whispers dwell,
Where stories of the heart compel.
A sonnet formed in silent cries,
  Beneath the stars, the truth lies.

The stillness hums a gentle tune,
Soft as the light of a waning moon.
In every pause, a breath of grace,
  A time to feel, a sacred space.

Each line, a sigh, a lover's kiss,
In absence found, a cherished bliss.
A silent song, the heart commands,
With muted dreams and open hands.

In shadows cast by twilight's glow,
We find the words we long to show.
A silent sonnet, soft and sweet,
In every heartbeat, love's heartbeat.

The Language of Rock

Veins of minerals, tales unfold,
In every crack, a story told.
With ancient whispers, time's design,
The language of rock, sublime, divine.

Granite grumbles, limestone sighs,
Each layer speaks, where wisdom lies.
From mountains high to valleys wide,
Nature's prose, a shifting tide.

Erosion weaves the timeless tale,
While rivers carve and storms prevail.
In every boulder, dreams collide,
The language of rock, our guide, allied.

In silence deep, the earth confides,
A symphony where history abides.
Let us listen and understand,
The silent scripts of this ancient land.

Chronicles Carved by Nature's Hand

Whispers of mountains, ancient and wise,
Rivers winding tales beneath the skies.
Trees stand tall, guardians of time,
Each leaf a story, each branch a rhyme.

Stone and water in a dance so grand,
Nature's palette, brushed by her hand.
Seasons shift in a graceful waltz,
In every crack and crevice, life exalts.

Caverns echo with forgotten lore,
History woven in the forest floor.
Sunsets cradle the day's last breath,
Nature uncovers her tales of death.

In every grain, a memory lies,
Carved by the years, beneath the skies.
Chronicles of beauty, fierce and bold,
In nature's embrace, stories are told.

The Art of Eternal Stillness

In the quiet of dawn, shadows softly creep,
Silent whispers of dreams, lulled to sleep.
Eternal stillness wraps the waking day,
Time pauses gently, holding breath at bay.

A canvas of calm, painted with light,
Moments suspended, pure and bright.
Ripples in ponds, a tranquil embrace,
Nature shares her gentle grace.

In the heart of the woods, silence reigns,
Echoes of peace flow through the veins.
Soft rustles of leaves, a sweet serenade,
In the art of stillness, worries fade.

Lost in the silence, the soul finds rest,
In stillness, we learn what we love best.
Eternal moments, fleeting yet true,
In the heart of the still, life starts anew.

Stone-etched Dreams of Yore

Granite whispers tales of the past,
Dreams etched deep, shadows cast.
Faded footprints of those long gone,
In the stillness, their spirits dawn.

Moss-covered legends, soft and green,
Nature's canvas where they've been.
The heart of the stone, a timekeeper's friend,
Each crack and crevice, a message to send.

Echoes of laughter, tears shed in grace,
Stone-etched dreams in this sacred place.
Time's fleeting fingers brush over the rock,
In silence, the memories gently unlock.

Beneath the surface, stories entwine,
Awakening visions both bold and divine.
Through stone and earth, we seek, explore,
For in the whispers of yore, dreams soar.

Landscapes of Immovable Thoughts

Thoughts like mountains, steadfast and grand,
Solid formations that willingly stand.
Through storms and shadows, they remain,
In the silence of peaks, no need for a chain.

Valleys of vision, wide and deep,
In the heart of reflection, secrets we keep.
Under the weight of sky and stone,
Immovable thoughts, we wander alone.

Rivers of reason carve through the land,
Flowing through moments that life has planned.
Mountains of wisdom, towering tall,
In landscapes of thought, we hear the call.

The horizon beckons with dreams yet to find,
In the stillness, we open our mind.
In every summit, in every fall,
Landscapes of thought, we gather them all.

Stony Ballads

In the silence where the stones lie,
Whispers of ancients softly sigh.
Each rock a tale of ages past,
Echoes of beauty, meant to last.

Through valleys deep and mountains high,
Nature sings a lullaby.
The gravel crunch beneath my feet,
A melody, both wild and sweet.

Underneath the midnight sky,
Stars like diamonds, twinkling shy.
Each twinkle tells a story grand,
Of time and space, a timeless band.

With hands of earth, we mold our fate,
From stony cold, we learn, create.
In every heart, a story beats,
In stony ballads, truth repeats.

Chronicles of the Crag

On rugged cliffs where eagles soar,
Chronicles of time, forevermore.
Whispers in the winds, they weave,
Stories that the mountains leave.

The sun casts shadows, long and bold,
On ancient stones, their stories told.
Resilience seen in every crack,
The struggle won, no turning back.

Mossy patches, green with grace,
Nature's painting, time won't erase.
Through the storms and fierce embrace,
The crags stand firm, a timeless space.

In every crevice, life does cling,
With stories waiting, soon to spring.
Chronicles echo, strong and clear,
Of craggy heights where dreams appear.

The Poetry of Earth

Beneath our feet, the stories breathe,
Voices of nature, weaves beneath.
The soil cradles life anew,
In every grain, a spark, a clue.

Mountains sing in their stoic grace,
Rivers dance, embracing space.
The storms may howl, the sun will shine,
In earth's vast canvas, all align.

Roots like fingers, grasp the ground,
Holding secrets, lost, yet found.
Life emerges, each vibrant hue,
The poetry of earth, ever true.

From oceans deep to sky so wide,
Nature's rhythms cannot hide.
In every moment, in every breath,
The poetry of life, defying death.

Embodied Legends

In the hearth of legends strong,
Whispers of the past belong.
Each figure carved from tales of yore,
Embodied legends, forevermore.

From ancient woods, to silent stones,
Heroes fought, their hearts like bones.
In twilight's glow, their shadows dance,
Carving paths of fate, by chance.

Through ages marked by time's embrace,
In every echo, we find our place.
The stories woven, rich and bold,
Embodied legends, dreams retold.

Each heartbeat holds a whisper sweet,
Legends live where souls meet.
In the fabric of our very being,
Embodied tales keep us believing.

Whispers of the Inanimate

In twilight's grasp, they softly sigh,
The chairs, the walls, they watch us cry.
Each corner keeps a silent tale,
Of joys and sorrows, dreams that pale.

The clock ticks slow, a steady beat,
While shadows dance on tired feet.
In every creak, a secret told,
Old memories, both warm and cold.

Beneath the dust, a life once shared,
The echoes linger, love declared.
Inanimate yet full of grace,
They hold the past, our timeless space.

A whisper here, a murmur there,
The objects hum with gentle care.
They witness all, from far and near,
These whispers of our hopes and fear.

Echoes in Granite

Upon the stones, the stories lay,
In rugged lines, they find their way.
Each chiseled face, a life embraced,
With weathered beauty, time interlaced.

In the quiet strength, a voice resides,
The mountain's heart, where spirit hides.
The echoes call from ages past,
A symphony, forever cast.

From fissures deep, the whispers rise,
In every crack, a truth defies.
Granite stands, both proud and tall,
A testament to life's grand thrall.

The sunrise paints the peaks aglow,
With colors rich, a vibrant show.
In every shade, the stories gleam,
Echoes in granite, a living dream.

Whispers Beneath the Surface

Beneath the waves, the secrets lie,
In depths where light can barely pry.
The currents speak in muted tones,
Through coral reefs and ancient stones.

With every ripple, whispers flow,
Of ships that sank, of tales we know.
Anemones sway, in graceful dance,
Echoing life in a tranquil trance.

The tides hold stories, draped in blue,
Of creatures lost and those anew.
In silken shadows, dreams emerge,
A world unseen begins to surge.

Bubbles rise, with laughter's sound,
As dolphins play, they leap, they bound.
Beneath the surface, life unfolds,
In whispers soft, the ocean holds.

Chiseled Echoes of Time

In marbled halls, the past does dwell,
With every statue, secrets swell.
The chisel's mark, a dance of light,
Each curve a story, crystal bright.

The echoes linger, softly fade,
In timeless art, where dreams are laid.
Through polished stone, the ages speak,
In every flaw, the strong and weak.

A world long gone, yet here it flows,
In chiseled forms, the spirit glows.
From shadows cast, they come alive,
In echoes deep, the memories thrive.

Remembered whispers, carved with care,
Resilient hearts in stillness stare.
The chiseled echoes, they shall remain,
A testament to joy and pain.

The Solid Symphony of the Ages

In whispers of the ancient trees,
The echoes dance with haunting ease.
Each note a tale from years gone by,
A melody that dares to fly.

The mountains hum in deep refrain,
With valleys softening every strain.
A symphony both grand and small,
In nature's grip, we hear it all.

The rivers flow, a swift caress,
Their laughter sings of old duress.
Through every crack and crevice wide,
The music of the earth abides.

A harmony of stone and breeze,
In timeless tunes that never cease.
With hearts attuned to life's embrace,
We join the dance of time and space.

Anchors of Memory in the Rough

In rugged shores, where tides have played,
The anchors of our dreams are laid.
Each stone, a witness to the fight,
A beacon in the darkest night.

The lighthouse stands, both bold and bright,
Guiding lost ships back to the light.
With every wave that breaks ashore,
Old memories whisper, evermore.

Through tempest winds and storms we face,
These anchors hold, our fleeting grace.
In nature's hand, we find our ground,
A steady pulse, a heart unbound.

So let us cast our fears away,
Embrace the night, await the day.
For in the rough, we find our way,
Anchors of hope, come what may.

Stone Shadows on the History Canvas

On ancient walls where echoes play,
The shadows of the past hold sway.
Each chipped and worn, a story told,
A canvas painted in hues of gold.

The carvings tell of love and woe,
Of battles fierce, of peace, and glow.
Each line a thread, each crack a path,
In stone's embrace, we feel the wrath.

As time unfolds its gentle hand,
The silent stones across the land.
Each shadow speaks of lives embraced,
In every mark, a trace of grace.

So let us pause and look around,
In stone's embrace, our truths are found.
For history holds a timeless glance,
In shadows cast, we find the dance.

The Voice of Pebbles Past

Beneath the surface, whispers lie,
The voice of pebbles, soft as sighs.
Each round and worn, a tale to share,
Of rivers crossed, of tranquil air.

With every step upon the shore,
Their stories rise, their wisdom sore.
From gentle streams to mighty seas,
The pebbles sing in subtle pleas.

In quiet moments, pause and hear,
Their songs bring strength, dissolve our fear.
A chorus rich, in timeless round,
The voice of nature, pure and sound.

So listen close to earth's soft call,
In every pebble, hear it all.
Their voices weave through time and space,
A melody of life's embrace.

Stonebound Chronicles

In the heart of the mountains, stones stand tall,
Whispers of time guard each rise and fall.
The tales they tell in silence profound,
Echoes of legends on hallowed ground.

With each shifting grain, a story unfolds,
Of battles and dreams that the earth firmly holds.
Their weathered faces bear scars of the years,
Chronicling laughter and drenching in tears.

Beneath the blue sky, they silently watch,
As seasons return and the world starts to notch.
Embracing the ages, they stand here to see,
Guardians of secrets, forever they'll be.

In shadows and sun, each stone finds its place,
A tapestry woven with memory's grace.
Though time may erode the strong and the brave,
The stones sing their songs, eternal and grave.

Rhymes of the Rocky Path

Upon the rocky path where dreams collide,
Nature's own chorus sings with each stride.
Footsteps in rhythm, the heartbeat of earth,
Marking the journey that gives life its worth.

Beneath the bright stars, the world feels so wide,
Listen, the mountains join in the tide.
Every sharp corner tells tales of the bold,
Adventures unfolding, their glory retold.

The wind carries whispers of joy and of pain,
A melody crafted by sun, snow, and rain.
Between stone and spirit, the harmony grows,
In the dance of the cosmos, the pathway just flows.

So wander with purpose, let echoes guide,
Embrace the wild rhythm, let shadows abide.
In each twist of the trail, find solace and trust,
For the rocky path leads to wonders robust.

Echoing Footsteps of the Past

In the stillness of nights, where shadows do creep,
Footsteps from yesteryear stir from their sleep.
Whispers of souls that once roamed these lands,
Stitching together their dreams with fine strands.

From echoes of laughter to cries of despair,
The past weaves a tapestry rich and rare.
Each footstep a story that longs to be heard,
In the silence of twilight, each dream becomes blurred.

The walls hold the secrets of lives intertwined,
Remnants of passions and hearts clearly aligned.
History whispers, etched deeply in stone,
The echoes remain, though the faces have flown.

Listen closely to the tales that they tell,
Of triumphs and trials within every shell.
Echoing footsteps through time gently drift,
A gift of remembrance, a timeless uploft.

Shadows on the Weathered Facade

On the weathered facade where shadows play,
Time dances lightly, an ancient ballet.
Carvings of moments, both bitter and sweet,
Merging together where lost pathways meet.

In strokes of the brush, the past comes alive,
Tracing the contours where memories strive.
Each shadow a memory, a flicker of light,
Creating a canvas where day kisses night.

Beneath the vast sky, where the old meets the new,
Time whispers its secrets, ever so true.
The stories are cast in each shadow that falls,
As life ebbs and flows, it forever calls.

In the twilight's embrace, the facade reveals,
The layers of history, with all that it feels.
Shadows of yesterday greet morning's first ray,
In the silence of dawn, night slowly gives way.

Songs of the Eternal Expanse

In skies so vast, the colors bloom,
Whispers of peace amid the gloom.
Stars hum a tune of ancient lore,
Their light a promise, forevermore.

Galaxies swirl in graceful dance,
Infinite tales of happenstance.
Each heartbeat echoes through the night,
Melodies born from cosmic light.

Winds carry songs from distant lands,
Softly they play, like tender hands.
A canvas rich with dreams untold,
Under the heavens, brave and bold.

Boundless and deep, where wild hearts soar,
In the expanse, we seek for more.
Together we sing, together we rise,
In the eternal, beneath the skies.

The Language of Solid Ground

Roots dig deep in the earth below,
Whispers of wisdom in every grow.
Mountains speak in silent tones,
Stones hold secrets, ancient bones.

Through valleys wide, the rivers flow,
Carving tales in a gentle show.
Each step we take on this sacred earth,
Reminds us of our shared rebirth.

Footprints echo on the dusty trails,
Stories linger where memory prevails.
We listen close to the land's refrain,
In every thunder, in every rain.

Grounded in truth, we find our place,
In the language of the solid grace.
With open hearts and lifted eyes,
We speak the earth, where wisdom lies.

Time's Embrace on Stony Shores

Waves crash soft on weathered stones,
Each whisper carries timeless tones.
Tides ebb and flow like life's own song,
In nature's arms, we all belong.

Sand between toes, we pause to breathe,
Moments woven, we dare to weave.
The horizon stretches, whispers of dreams,
A tapestry woven in sunlit beams.

Seagulls call with voices clear,
Their cries are echoes we hold dear.
In stillness found on stony shores,
Time's embrace, forever endures.

Under the sky's vast, loving dome,
Each heartbeat tells us we are home.
As stars appear, we find our peace,
In time's embrace, we are released.

Reflections in Weathered Stone

Grit and grace in textures shown,
Each crack a tale, each line a bone.
Silent stories linger there,
Within the stone, memories share.

The sun's warm touch on rugged faces,
Illuminates time's fleeting traces.
Nature's canvas, rich and bold,
In every weathered inch, behold.

Crevices hold the whispers of time,
Echoes of ages in rhythmic rhyme.
We pause to ponder, to understand,
The beauty found in nature's hand.

In the stones, we find our way,
Reflections of life, night and day.
With open hearts, we honor the past,
In weathered stone, our futures cast.

Eternal Echoes

In the silence of the night,
Whispers dance on silver beams.
Memories cling to the shadows,
Carried forth by gentle dreams.

Footsteps linger, soft and light,
Echos of a time long past.
Through the corridors of thought,
The moments fade yet hold fast.

Each heartbeat sings a melody,
Woven deep in heart and soul.
In the echoes, we find solace,
A reminder of being whole.

Through the ages, voices call,
In every sigh, in every breath.
Eternal is the bond we share,
Even beyond the veil of death.

Carved Whispers

Amidst the trees, a story lies,
Carved in bark, a tale untold.
Whispers of the ancient woods,
In every line, a piece of gold.

Beneath a sky of endless blue,
Echoes of the past resound.
In the rustling leaves, they speak,
Secrets that the winds have found.

Every hollow, every groove,
Holds a truth, a fleeting glance.
Nature's voice, a gentle guide,
In its rhythm, we find our dance.

So let us tread with quiet steps,
And listen closely, heart in hand.
For in the whispers of the earth,
We discover where we stand.

Etched Dreams

In the canvas of the night sky,
Stars etch stories with their light.
Wishes dance like fireflies,
Flickering in the quiet night.

Through the moments we sketch and draw,
Dreams unfold in colors bright.
Each thought a brush, each heartbeat true,
Painting life in shades of flight.

As dawn awakens, shadows fade,
But dreams remain in corners deep.
Etched in hearts, they breathe and swell,
Whispering secrets as we sleep.

Let us cherish what we dream,
For from our hopes, great tales arise.
Etched in time, they guide our way,
Transforming all beneath the skies.

Shadows of Time

Beneath the moon's soft silver glow,
Shadows stretch across the floor.
In every corner, a story lurks,
Woven thick with age and more.

Faces flicker in the dark,
Echoes of those who came before.
Their laughter lingers, caught in air,
In the silence, we explore.

Time stands still in whispered breaths,
Memories cast on fragile walls.
We wander through the shadows deep,
Listening to the twilight calls.

With every step, a thread is spun,
Connecting us to yesterday.
In the shadows, we are anchored,
Guided through the fray.

Milton Keynes UK
Ingram Content Group UK Ltd.
UKHW022006091024
449514UK00007B/65

9 789916 881101